Emotionally Unavailable, But Make It Poetic

55 poems and not one of them solves anything

Tim Stoodley

Copyright © 2025 Tim Stoodley
All rights reserved.
No part of this publication may be reproduced, stored in a retrieval system, or transmitted in any form or by any means, electronic, mechanical, photocopying, recording, or otherwise, without the prior written permission of the author, except in the case of brief quotations used in reviews, articles, or academic analysis.

ISBN: 979-8-316-47808-8

This is a work of creative nonfiction. Any resemblance to real persons, living or dead, is purely coincidental. Probably.
Please don't steal these. The poems have trust issues already.

For you xx

Disclaimer:
This book contains traces of hope, sarcasm, emotional spirals, and poor meal planning advice.
Please do not attempt to diagnose yourself using poetry.
Side effects may include sighing, nodding, or texting your ex.
Read responsibly.

Emotionally Unavailable, But Make It Poetic

CONTENTS

Contents (you're literally here)	i
Unhelpful Prologue	ii
Everything's a Bit Much	1
Oh No	27
Maybe?	49
That'll Do	67

This isn't a deep, life-changing poetry book.

You're not going to find enlightenment, inner peace, or an inspiring quote to get tattooed on your ribs.
What you will find is 55 (ish) poems written by someone who overthinks for sport and copes with humour, naps, and the occasional existential spiral.

These poems cover things like:
- Anxiety
- Burnout
- Love
- Grief
- Fatherhood
- Beige food
- Cancelled plans
- Whatever emotion happens when your favourite mug is in the dishwasher

Some are serious. Some are stupid. Some accidentally rhyme. Most were written when I should've been doing literally anything else.

I've split them into four parts to make it feel like I had a plan (I didn't):
- **Everything's a Bit Much** – the classic mental breakdown section
- **Oh No** – the heartbreak/grief/emotional sucker-punch zone
- **Maybe?** – where things start to feel slightly less awful
- **That'll Do** – joy, sarcasm, carbs, and emotional growth (but low effort)

There's no moral. No grand message. Just a bunch of poems that might make you feel seen, laugh a bit, or go *"yep, same."*

And honestly? That'll do for me.

EVERYTHING'S A BIT MUCH

The brain won't shut up. The body's knackered. The world's a lot.
These poems sit in the fog, overthinking, underfunctioning,
wondering what happened to that optimistic version of you who once
bought vitamins.

Razorblade Mind

There's a razor in my mind,
not in my hand,
No silver glint, no crimson drip,
just thoughts too sharp to withstand.

It carves through every memory,
whispers twisted, cruel,
Shaving down my worth to dust,
Grinding logic into fuel.

It slashes with regrets unsaid,
incisions laced with doubt,
I try to stitch the wounds with hope,
but the stitches all fall out.

No bandage stops a phantom blade,
no scream can dull its edge,
And every time I try to fight,
it carves me closer to the ledge.

There's a razor in my mind,
and I know its every scar,
But maybe if I drop the blade,
it won't cut quite as far.

Still Breathing, Not Living

Do you ever feel like you're still breathing,
but you stopped living?
Like your body's a clock,
tick-tick-ticking,
but the hands are stuck?

The alarm goes off.
You rise.
You move.
You function.
You answer emails and eat cereal for dinner,
but the spark,
the *you*,
is on permanent holiday,
somewhere you'll never afford to visit.

"Cheer up," they say,
as if sadness were a misplaced set of keys.
But this isn't something you find
under the sofa.
It is the sofa.
Heavy.
Grey.
Immovable.
And it feels like you're sinking into it,
one lost thought at a time.

You laugh sometimes,
because it's easier than explaining
why your soul feels like it's buffering.
The loading wheel of existence spins,
but nothing ever downloads.

You used to dream big.
Now you dream of being enough.
Of feeling joy without suspicion.
Imagine that, a day
where smiling doesn't feel like treason.

But here's the thing about breathing:
it's a rhythm.
And even when it feels pointless,
that rhythm keeps you here.
It's the song of life whispering,
"Don't give up. Not just yet."

Because even when the spark feels gone,
it's only hiding,
waiting for the smallest flicker of hope
to bring it roaring back.

You're still breathing,
and that means something.
It means you've survived every bad day,
every dark night,
and you're still here to see
what tomorrow might bring.

The tunnel?
It's real, and it's long,
but there's light ahead,
and it's waiting for you,
not because you've earned it,
but because you deserve it.

So hold on. Please.
Not just to survive,
but to live.
Because one day,
you'll laugh,
and it won't feel forced.
You'll smile,
and it will reach your eyes.
You'll breathe,
and it will feel like freedom.

That day is coming.
Keep breathing until it does.

Echoes in My Mind

In the quiet of the night, the whispers rise,
Threads of thought unraveling, no disguise.
Every doubt I've ever known
Creeps in to claim me, alone.

I wrestle shadows I can't see,
Ghosts that linger, haunting me.

I'm torn between the silence and the storm,
A tug of war I've fought so long.
The voices echo loud, they tear my soul,
Pulling me down a hole I can't control.

Each step forward feels like a fall,
Questions haunt, they build a wall.
I try to break free, but they hold tight,
Binding me to a sleepless night.

I scream, but no one hears a sound,
A captive here, I'm shackled, bound.
Drowning in an endless sea,
Wondering who I'm meant to be.

If I could find a way to set me free
From these shadows that won't let me be.
But here I stand, my mind at war,
Holding on to who I was before.

Everyone Feels Sad Sometimes

Everyone feels sad sometimes, they say,
But for me, sadness never goes away.
It's not a passing cloud, not just rain,
It's the sky, the air, a constant strain.

People ask why, but there's no one thing,
No tragedy or tale with a sting,
Just an endless grey where blue should be,
A quiet ache, a missing key.

Why do they feel sad sometimes,
Yet I'm left with sadness as my only rhyme?
This discontent, my normal, my state,
A heavy cloak, an accepted weight.

Yes, everyone feels sad now and then,
But sadness feels like my only friend.
So I walk through days in silent prose,
With dreams unopened, eyes half-closed,

And wonder, as others dance in light,
If my world will ever feel that bright.

Kinda Tired

Kinda tired
being okay with things
I'm not okay with,
the words I swallow,
the silent agreements,
the nods, the small laughs,
as if I'm fine, as if it doesn't burn.

There's a weight to silence,
a sharpness to pretending,
and each time I let it go
it feels like letting go of me,
a small piece lost,
one I'll never get back.

I wonder how many times
I've said, "It's fine" when it wasn't,
how often I've let things slide,
let myself disappear
just to keep the peace,
to keep the world steady,
even as I stumble.

Kinda tired of watching my life
from a step removed,
like I'm playing the part
someone else wrote,
wearing a smile that doesn't fit,
in scenes I barely believe.

One day, maybe,
I'll stop nodding, stop bending,
let the words come out raw and unpolished.
For now, though,
I keep going,
kinda tired,
kinda here,
kinda not.

I Bet You're Lonely

I bet you're lonely.
You picked up this book,
Found this poem,
Because you're lonely.

It's like I can see you through the pages,
See into your soul.
Hurts, doesn't it?
Being called out by some grey-haired bloke you've never met.

I bet you flinched,
Just a little.
Like I'd cracked open a door
You thought was locked.

Maybe you'll scoff,
Tell yourself I'm wrong,
That you just like poetry,
That you're fine, really.

But we both know the truth,
Don't we?

Silence gets heavy at night,
Like a coat too thick for summer,
Like a whisper that turns into a scream.
You fill the void with screens,
With noise,
With anything but the sound
Of your own thoughts.

And yet, here you are,
Letting a stranger's voice
Sit beside you for a while.

Maybe that's enough.
Maybe it isn't.
But at least, for this moment,
You're not alone.

You Know What Your Problem Is?

You know what your problem is?
You think overthinking is helping you.
Like if you just replay it enough,
you'll crack the code.
Make the right call.
Avoid the fall.

You tell yourself it's strategy.
That dissecting every word they said
will somehow stop you from getting hurt again.
That worrying about the future
will cushion the blow when it finally arrives.

But it won't.
It never has.

You're not preparing,
you're paralysing.
You're stuck in the same scene,
on a loop you wrote yourself.
And the worst part?
You call it control.

Here's the truth:
No amount of thinking
will ever make life certain.
There's no formula
that guarantees the outcome.
No mental rehearsal
that stops things from breaking.

Sometimes the answer
isn't in thinking.
It's in *doing*.

Emotionally Unavailable, But Make It Poetic

You don't need another pro/con list.
You don't need another sleepless night.
You need to move.
Act.
Live.

Stop trying to solve a problem
that only exists in your head.
Stop rewriting conversations
that already ended.
Stop rehearsing pain
you haven't even felt yet.

This isn't clarity.
It's fear wearing a lab coat.

So here's your way out:
Make the decision.
Take the step.
Let it be messy.
Let it be wrong.
Let it be *real*.

Because life doesn't happen in your head.
It happens when you show up for it.

Because He's a Guy

He staves himself,
He cuts his wrist,
But this little story has a twist.

He hates himself,
He wants to die,
You can see that by the look in his eyes.

You think this is crazy?
You think it's a lie?
Of course you do,

Because he's a guy.

Is the Fish Afraid of the Shark?

Does a fish get anxious about the shark?
Does it spend its days
hiding behind coral,
waiting for the worst?

Does it spiral into "what ifs"
when the water ripples wrong?
"What if it's coming?
What if it's close?
What if this is it?"

Or does it just swim,
because swimming is all it knows?

I wish I could be like that.
Unbothered by the currents.
Not questioning every shadow,
every small splash.

But here I am,
panicking over emails,
over parking spaces,
over how my voice sounded
in a conversation from two weeks ago.

The fish doesn't replay its near misses,
wondering if it could've swum better,
faster,
smarter.
It just swims.

Meanwhile, I'm stuck
in an ocean of nonsense,
fearing storms that never come,
watching for sharks that don't exist.

Maybe the fish knows something I don't.
Maybe it understands
that danger isn't the same as fear.
That survival doesn't have to feel
like drowning.

So tomorrow, I'll try.
I'll swim through my own currents,
even if my mind is screaming.
Because if a fish can face the open sea
and still keep moving,
then maybe,
just maybe,
so can I.

When Am I Meant to Feel Like an Adult?

They said by thirty-five, I'd have it all,
A house with a garden, a career to enthrall.
But my rent eats my paycheck, my dreams on delay,
And the plants on my windowsill die in a day.

Mum had two kids, Dad built the shed,
I'm just out here trying to get out of bed.
I've mastered my coffee, but not my own mind,
Anxiety's the roommate I can't leave behind.

"When am I meant to feel like an adult?"
My inner monologue, a running insult.
"You should have savings, a pension, a plan!"
But my plan's Netflix and avoiding the man.

A house? Don't be daft, I can't even buy toast,
A takeaway's a luxury I envy the most.
Mum's mortgage was cheaper than my parking space,
Yet they tell me it's effort, not a rigged rat race.

They said adulthood's freedom, but here's what I see:
Emails, insurance, and lost Wi-Fi keys.
The to-do list gets longer, my patience runs thin,
Where do I even begin to begin?

Sometimes I laugh, 'cause what else can you do?
The worlds on fire, but my kettle is too.
I'm stuck in a cycle of memes and despair,
Still wishing for holidays I'll never quite snare.

But maybe, just maybe, that's not the whole tale,
Success isn't linear, nor measured on scales.
We're all winging it, faking the part,
Doing our best with a scrappy, full heart.

Emotionally Unavailable, But Make It Poetic

So here's to the chaos, the mess, and the dread,
To the nights we can't sleep, overthinking in bed.
Maybe adulthood's not what they told us to chase,
It's finding small joys in this maddening race.

When am I meant to feel like an adult?
Who knows? Maybe never. That's no one's fault.
I'll stumble and trip, but I'll still make my way,
One coffee, one meltdown, one meme at a day.

Whispers of the Worm

There's a worm in my head,
A relentless writhing presence,
A whisperer of doubts,
A gnawing truth I bury between layers of practised stoicism.

As a man, I am to stand tall,
Broad-shouldered and unshaken,
Expected to march through the day
With purpose and certainty.

I am to crack on,
As though there is no storm within,
As if the sky isn't constantly
On the verge of breaking.

The worm never sleeps,
He coils tighter in moments of silence,
Feeding on the smallest fear,
Growing fat on my unspoken worry.

He tells me that I am weak,
That this quiet battle is mine alone,
Unseen, unacknowledged,
Yet always present.

I smile through, my face a mask of calm,
My words steady, practised.
Inside I am a battlefield,
The clash of self-doubt against the façade of strength.

I must act like nothing is happening,
Maintain the illusion of composure,
Even as the worm thrashes,
Demanding my attention, begging for release.

Emotionally Unavailable, But Make It Poetic

Nobody sees the tremors beneath my skin,
The way my heart races against the cage of my ribs.
They see a man who is steadfast,
Unyielding to the invisible storm.

Not knowing the effort it takes
To keep the worm hidden,
To pretend it isn't there.
And so, I carry on.

Silent in my struggle,
The weight of expectations heavy,
The worms whisper a constant companion,
I crack on, for that is what I must do.

Even if the worm
Never gives me a break,
I will push forward still,
For this battle is mine to take.

When Did I Sign Up for This?

They said adulthood would come naturally.
Like puberty, but with better clothes and a mortgage.
Yet here I am, staring at my bank balance,
wondering if I can afford electricity *and* cheese this month.

My parents bought a house at my age.
I bought a scented candle just to feel something.
They had three kids.
I have three streaming subscriptions
and a pile of unopened post labelled "Urgent."

Is this the life they meant?
Filling out forms I don't understand,
Googling "How to sound assertive in emails,"
and panicking over a mystery direct debit?

The big secret is no one knows what they're doing.
But they're better at faking it.
I still feel like a teenager in disguise,
hoping no one notices I don't belong
in the aisle with the serious bread.

What even is a credit score?
Why is everyone obsessed with pensions?
I can barely commit to dinner plans,
let alone a 40-year savings strategy.

But hey, at least I'm consistent.
Consistently late.
Consistently stressed.
Consistently arguing with the toaster
because it's definitely *not* set to incinerate.

Maybe adulthood isn't about having it together.
Maybe it's about pretending you do.
About laughing at the chaos,
knowing the kettle will boil eventually.

Because let's be honest,
no one's got it all figured out.
Not even the people who own houses.
They're just as confused,
but with better carpets.

So here's to the mess,
the overdrafts, the bad decisions,
and the ever-growing pile of Tupperware lids
that don't fit any containers.

Adulthood's a scam.
But at least we're all in on it together.

I Give It Everything

I give it everything.
Not just the hours,
the early starts, the broken nights,
but parts of myself
most people never see.

I give it my health.
Trading sleep for shifts,
meals for moments in the cab
between one emergency
and the next.
There are weeks I feel like
I'm more uniform than person.

I give it my days off.
CPD courses, court statements,
chasing paperwork
when I'd rather be chasing rest.
Even on my own time,
I'm never all the way switched off.

I give it my empathy.
To strangers who are scared,
to patients in pain,
to people who've lost everything
by the time I arrive.
I meet them in their worst hour
and offer whatever peace I can carry.

I give it my social battery.
I miss birthdays,
My daughter's school plays,
I cancel plans,
pull away without meaning to.
Some days, I've used up all my words
before I even get home.

Emotionally Unavailable, But Make It Poetic

I give it my relationships,
watched good people walk away
because they couldn't carry
what this job leaves me holding.
Because sometimes I come home
and don't know how to put it all down.

I give it my mental health.
Not all at once,
but bit by bit,
in quiet moments
after tough calls
that stay with me longer than they should.

And still,
I show up.

Because I love this job.

I love what it stands for.
I love the honour of walking into chaos
and bringing calm.
Of being trusted
when someone's world is falling apart.

It takes from me, yes,
but it gives me purpose,
perspective,
pride.

I give it everything.
And somehow,
there's always something left in me
to give again.

Because I'm a paramedic.
And I wouldn't be anything else.

Poems Are Meant to Rhyme

Poems are meant to rhyme.
But what if there's no word to describe what you need to describe?
No words to tell the story.
What if finding stupid little rhymes uses brain power that you just don't have?

See poems are meant to rhyme so they're easy to listen to.
Easy to follow. Easy to picture.
But what if the picture you're painting can't be followed?
What if you're not rhyming buttercups and fairy cakes?

Yeah, maybe people will listen,
If I rhyme about roses, about sunsets and rainbows too.
But why must it be dressed in rhyme to be seen as true?
Why polish pain, make it pretty, just for you?

So, poems are meant to rhyme so they're easy to listen to eh?
Maybe rhyming poems will mean people start listening to me, yay?
Perhaps I'll throw in some little ditties about flowers.
Yeah, then people will be listening to me, for hours.

So I'm rhyming about the shitty blackness that consumes my soul.
You want it to rhyme? I'll play the role.
Does this sound better, make it happier in your mind.
I'll dig up daisies from the darkness, see what I can find.

Yeah, I'll try this rhyming shit, maybe people will find it easier to listen.
Been telling folks for years, begging for some recognition.

Truth is, it doesn't matter if I rhyme the words.
Or try to explain what's in my head.
Because it's funny, isn't it?
People only hear you when you're *dead*.

The Lighthouse

I used to think being a lighthouse
was something to be proud of.
Steady.
Seen.
Useful.

I lit up the dark
so others didn't crash.
Warned them off rocks
I'd hit a thousand times myself.

I stood still
while storms tore past.
Didn't flinch.
Didn't ask for shelter.
Didn't ask for anything.

And people noticed,
sort of.
They said things like,
"You're so strong."
Like it was a compliment.
Like it wasn't a warning sign
I was flashing in Morse code:
HELP ME.

But no one checks on the lighthouse.
Not really.
They assume you're fine
because you're still standing.
Because your light's still on.
Because your cracks
look architectural.

You can get tired, even standing still.
You can feel your own bricks loosening.

Emotionally Unavailable, But Make It Poetic

You can wonder what it would be like
to turn the light off
just for one night.

Not out of spite.
Not because you want ships to crash.
Just to see what silence feels like
when it's yours.

The worst part?
Even when I'm crumbling,
people still steer by me.
Still say "I knew I could count on you."
And I nod,
because it's easier
than explaining the erosion.

But I've started thinking
maybe lighthouses weren't meant to stand alone.
Maybe the strongest thing I can do
is let someone inside.
Even if they track in sand.
Even if they see the rust.

I don't want to guide anymore.
Not always.
I want to sit on the shoreline with someone
and watch the waves
without having to save them.

Stop Fighting Ghosts

Do you ever lose a battle
that only exists in your head?
Like you're shadowboxing words
I never even said?

You read my texts like tea leaves,
searching for hidden meaning.
I say "I'm fine,"
but you think I mean
everything's crumbling, and it's your fault.

You rewrite conversations
until they barely resemble the truth,
like a novelist spinning plots
out of silence.

I see it,
the way your mind spirals,
grabbing hold of every "what if"
and turning it into "what must be."

And I get it.
I do.
Your brain's trying to protect you
from a hurt that isn't there.
But here's the thing:
I can't compete with all that.

I can't fight the ghosts you've conjured,
the villains you've imagined me to be.
I can only stand here,
hands open,
offering you reality.

I'm not here to hurt you.
I'm not hiding some secret meaning
in the pause between my words.
Sometimes, a pause is just a pause.

So let go of the battles
you're fighting in your mind.
Let me in,
messy, unpolished,
real.

Because I'd rather sit in your silence
than watch you drown
in the noise you create.

OH NO

Here come the ghosts.
The heartbreaks you thought you'd processed.
The grief that arrives uninvited.
The memories that show up in smells, songs, and strangers on trains.
These poems don't wallow, but they *do* ache, in that quiet way you
only notice when the kettle's boiling and no one's speaking.

Give Me a Reason to Hate You

I wish you'd done me dirty.
I wish I had the proof,
a stranger's name, a whispered lie,
some cracks beneath the truth.

I wish I'd caught you out one night,
your phone face-down, your tone,
some half-assed tale you couldn't sell
that let me hate you whole.

But no.
You loved me right.
You loved me *soft*.
And then you let me go.
No slammed doors, no screaming match,
just silence, pure and slow.

You didn't cheat, you didn't lie,
you just stopped feeling *us*.
And now I'm stuck inside the ache
with no one left to trust.

I wish you'd given me a scar,
something deep, sharp and clear,
instead of all these memories
I still keep holding near.

You're not the villain in my head,
you're every perfect part.
And that's the cruelest ending yet:
to lose you...
but not my heart.

The Leaving Before Goodbye

I don't think it's the moment they leave that hurts the most.
It's when you realise
they'd been walking away in small, silent steps
long before the door ever closed.

It's in the way their smile
started showing up late
and never quite reached their eyes.
How their laughter used to fill the room,
then shrank to something polite and distant,
like it didn't recognise you anymore.

You start replaying moments like an old film reel,
pausing to study the frames,
Was it *this* look?
That reply?
The hug that felt more like a pat on the back
than a promise to stay?

It's not the silence after they're gone that shatters you.
It's the silence that wrapped itself around you
while they were still sat next to you,
scrolling their phone,
smiling at someone else's world,
while yours was slowly falling apart.

You were inches from them,
yet it felt like shouting across a canyon.
You reached out,
but your hands came back empty.

You told yourself stories to cope:
Maybe they're tired.
Maybe you're too much.
Maybe it's just a phase.
But deep down, you knew,

People don't disappear all at once.
They evaporate.
They fade.
They slip through your fingers
like mist you were never meant to hold.

And the worst part?
You noticed.

You noticed the shift.
The change in temperature.
The way their love turned lukewarm
while yours stayed burning.

And still,
you stayed.
Hoping they'd circle back.
Hoping you could anchor them.
Hoping the version of them you loved
was still tucked inside somewhere,
waiting to return.

But love doesn't rewind.
And now you're left
cradling memories like fragile glass,
sharp and reflective,
full of someone who no longer exists.

A version of them that's already gone.
And a version of you
that still believed
they wouldn't be.

Not All Soulmates Stay

They say soulmates stay.
That they're the ones who last,
who grow old with you,
who finish your sentences and
make the tea just right.

But not all soulmates are forever.
Some are flash-floods,
some are wildfires,
intense, unstoppable,
beautiful,
brief.

Some arrive
like they've been coming your whole life.
No warning.
No plan.
Just a sudden knowing,
oh, there you are.

They make the world softer,
your laugh louder,
your heart feel like it's found its home.

And you think,
this has to be it.
This has to be the one who stays.

But some soulmates aren't meant to stay.
Some are meant
to shake you awake.
To pull you back to yourself.
To remind you
that your heart still works.
That you still feel.
That love isn't always safe,
but it's always worth it.

Emotionally Unavailable, But Make It Poetic

They don't leave because it wasn't real.
They leave
because they've done what they came to do.
And that,
that's the hardest kind of love.

The kind that ends
not because it was broken,
but because it was *complete*.

A whole story
in half the pages.

And you'll ache.
God, you'll ache.
For a future that never got written.
For a version of life
where you got to keep them.

But hear this,
just because they didn't stay,
doesn't mean they weren't yours.

They were. Fully.
Undeniably.

They left fingerprints on your soul.
They carved laughter into your bones.
They changed the way you love.
The way you *are*.

And maybe that's what a soulmate really is.
Not someone who stays,
but someone who shows you
what love *can* feel like.

Even if it was only
for a moment.

Even if it hurts
to remember.

Fading Echoes

One day, someone will think of you for the last time.
Not because they chose to forget,
But because time is a quiet thief,
Stealing even the faces we swore we'd never let go.

The way you laughed,
The way you said their name,
The little moments that once felt like everything.
They will fade.
Little by little,
Until you are nothing more than a distant echo,
Buried beneath a life that moved on without you.

And the same will happen to you.
The people you love now,
The ones who make your world feel full,
Who make you feel safe, alive, understood.
One day, without realising it,
You'll think of them for the last time.

And that's the cruelest part of life.
Not just that it ends,
But that it keeps going.
That people disappear from our stories
Long before they disappear from this world.

We chase the next thing, the next moment,
Never realising that what we have right now
Is the very thing we will one day ache for.

So before time takes it from you,
Pay attention.
Look them in the eyes.
Hold them a little longer.
Speak the words you're afraid to say.

Emotionally Unavailable, But Make It Poetic

Love the people in front of you
Like you won't get another chance.

Because one day,
You won't.

I Swear, I Didn't Mean to Hurt You

I broke your heart, but not on purpose,
I was reckless, not ruthless, I swear.
Like tripping and spilling red wine on a carpet,
And realising… mate, that's never coming out.

I fumbled with love like car keys in the dark,
Dropped us between the seats.
I swore I'd pick us up later,
But later came with a bus fare instead.

You wanted poetry, I gave you punchlines,
You needed roots, I gave you wings,
I was the cold side of the pillow,
Comforting, but never really warm.

And now, I see it,
In the echo of words I can't take back,
In the space where your laugh used to be,
In the texts I don't send but still type.

I didn't mean to hurt you,
Like a bad haircut or an awkward hug,
Like saying "you too" when the waiter says "enjoy your meal."
And yet, there it is.

If I could rewind, I'd rewrite the script,
Make myself softer where I was sharp,
Make my love a little louder,
And my fears a little quiet.

But love isn't an Etch A Sketch,
You don't just shake it and start again.
So here I am,
Standing in the mess I made,
Hoping time forgives me,
Even if you don't.

Tonight

The thing I am missing most about you tonight:

~~Boobs~~

Snuggles.

Queuing Behind Someone Who Smells Like Her

It happens in Sainsbury's.
Frozen aisle.
A woman in a navy jumper
smells exactly like the one
I used to love.

That same shampoo-perfume-deodorant mix,
like citrus and something warm,
soft.
It hits me before I can place it.
Then I do.
And it knocks the air out of me.

She's just standing there,
debating oven pizza,
and I'm behind her
trying not to think about
Sunday mornings,
deep chats,
and that laugh that made me feel
like I was getting away with something.

It's mad,
how scent can pull you backwards
without asking permission.
No warning. No consent.
Just,
here she is,
in someone else's skin.

Not all of her.
Just pieces.
The nape of her neck.
The smile in her voice.
The way she used to steal the duvet
like she was entitled to warmth.

Emotionally Unavailable, But Make It Poetic

I pretend to care deeply about frozen peas
while my chest does that thing
where it forgets how to be casual.

Eventually,
she walks off,
pizza in hand.
And I stay there,
weirdly gutted,
like I've just bumped into a version of myself
I thought I'd outgrown.

Because isn't that the thing about ghosts?
They never look like themselves.
They turn up
in strangers
on a Tuesday
when your guard is down.

And for a moment,
you remember
exactly why you loved her.

And exactly
why you had to stop.

I Miss Saying Goodnight to You

I miss saying goodnight to you,
the simple hush of it,
the way it folded the day
like a soft blanket over our tired thoughts.

I miss the pause
before the silence,
your voice dimmed by sleep,
mumbling something half-sweet, half-unfinished,
like a secret only dreams could hold.

It wasn't grand,
not some cinematic thing.
Just a soft "goodnight"
in the glow of a screen,
or across a pillow,
or through a phone
already half-asleep in my hand.

I didn't know it would be the last one.
Nobody ever does.

Now, the nights stretch longer,
no punctuation, no end.
Just the hum of my thoughts
where your voice used to be.

And it's strange,
how what I miss
isn't the big moments,
but the smallest one,
said soft, said often, said without thinking.

I miss saying goodnight to you.
And I miss
being the one
you said it to.

Goodnight, you.

The Shape of Grief

Grief doesn't scream.
It whispers.
It waits.
It settles in the space they left
and rearranges fate.

It's reaching for your phone,
then pulling your hand away.
It's hearing their song
in a shop aisle,
and forgetting how to stay.

It's the laugh you almost shared,
the one that fades too soon.
It's the echo of a voice
that won't return to fill the room.

Grief wears no black.
It hides in light,
in morning cups of tea.
In jokes they'd love,
in news you'd tell,
if only they could see.

It's love without direction,
a tide without a shore.
A thousand quiet moments
that ache a little more.

You don't "get over" losing them.
You fold them into you.
In how you speak, in how you walk,
in all you say and do.

It never leaves completely.
It softens, then it stays,
not as weight,
but as a shadow
that walks beside your days.

One More Time

Isn't it strange how we never quite see
The moments that matter, the ones that just *be?*
They pass like a whisper, they feel so small,
Yet later, we realise they were everything, all.

The laughter at midnight, the hum of a song,
The feeling that nothing could possibly go wrong.
A look from a friend, a seat at the table,
The sense you belonged there, safe and stable.

We never know when it's the very last time,
The final group photo, the throwaway line,
The voice that once called you, so steady and clear,
Becomes just an echo you ache now to hear.

The "everyday" moments, the ones we let slide,
Are the ones that come flooding when years have gone by.
And when you're alone with a memory or two,
You'll wish you had noticed what time never drew.

Not to change anything, not to rewrite,
But to hold it again, just one more night.
To feel that soft peace in a world so wide,
Before life pulled you over to the other side.

So, pause while you're in it, don't race through the day,
Look around softly before it slips away.
Because one day you'll long for the life that you knew,
Not to fix it,
Just to feel it,
One more time through.

The Spaces Between

I look at my hands,
at the gaps between my fingers.
That's where yours fit perfectly.

It's strange, isn't it?
How something as small as touch
can feel like the answer
to questions I never knew I was asking.

Your hand in mine
isn't just fingers and palms.
It's steadiness in the storm,
a quiet kind of magic.

We fit,
not like puzzle pieces,
because puzzles are rigid,
meant to lock together
and stay still.

No.
We're more like
waves and shorelines,
meeting, pulling,
changing each other with every touch.

And sometimes,
I catch myself tracing those spaces,
the gaps where your fingers rest.
I think about how they're empty
when you're not here,
and how full
the whole world feels
when you are.

Emotionally Unavailable, But Make It Poetic

I used to think love
was fireworks,
big, loud,
impossible to miss.
But now I know,
it's in the spaces.
The gaps.
The quiet.

It's in the way our hands meet,
perfectly,
like they always knew
where they belonged.

The Nicest People

Why is it always the nicest people who end up the loneliest?
The ones who text back quickly.
The ones who remember your birthday.
The ones who ask how you are,
and actually want to hear the answer.

They care too much.
Feel too deeply.
Love too hard.

They give and give,
thinking it's what people do when they care.
But not everyone gives back.
Not everyone holds your heart as gently as you handed it to them.

So these people,
the warm ones,
the kind ones,
they start to disappear.

Not dramatically.
No big farewell.
They just... stop showing up.
They start spending weekends in,
walking solo through city streets,
eating dinner with only their thoughts for company.

And they tell themselves it's better this way.
That solitude is safer.
That silence doesn't disappoint.

But after a while,
they try again.

They dip their toes back into the world.
Meet new people. Laugh at new jokes.
And this time,
they don't hand over the whole map.
They keep something for themselves.

They're still kind,
but now with boundaries.
Still loving,
but not blind to red flags.

They become a little tougher,
a little quieter,
a little more *them*.

And people say,
"You've changed."

But that's the point.

Because now they choose peace over pleasing.
Truth over tolerance.
Depth over company.

They may still feel lonely sometimes.
But not in the way they used to.

Because now,
they're no longer surrounded by people
who make them feel unseen.

Now, they're alone by choice.
Not because they're broken.
But because they've learned to protect
what made them kind in the first place.

The Last Time

There was no slow fade,
no curtain call,
no grown-up voice
saying, *"this is the end."*

Just a bike left leaning in a garage,
mud on your shoes,
sunset sweat drying on your neck
as you ran inside
for dinner.

Just another ordinary day
that quietly closed a door
you didn't know you'd never open again.

No one tells you
that one day will be the last time,
the last time you'll sprint barefoot
down a cul-de-sac
pretending lava's at your heels,
the last time you'll believe
a stick can be a sword,
or that you're being chased
by something
only your imagination can see.

The last time you'll play
without thinking about how you look,
or what's next,
or if this moment
is worth remembering.

And that's the thing,
you didn't know to hold on tighter.
You didn't know
to make it count.

Emotionally Unavailable, But Make It Poetic

You just went to bed,
smelling like outside,
full of laughter and cereal
and summer air.
You didn't know
that life had already moved on.

And now,
you chase memories
like you once chased monsters,
hoping to catch
even one
before it slips
into the quiet.

MAYBE?

Something shifts.
It's not a miracle, but it's enough to notice.
These poems hold resilience, connection, softness, and the beautiful awkwardness of still being here.
There's a bit of love in this part. A bit of trying.
It's messy, but kind.

Phoebe.

I knew you first by silence,
the pause before the cry,
a flicker in the universe
that dared to say, *I'll try*.

Then came the world in colour,
your breath against my chest,
a storm of need and gentleness
that woke me from the rest.

I watched you grow in inches,
in questions and in grace,
each scrape upon your little knees
etched soft upon my face.

You wore my coats like mountains,
my shoes like foreign lands,
and every dream you stumbled through
was steadied by my hands.

I've held you in the silence,
and braved your fiercest storm,
stood outside your pre-teen walls
still hoping you'd feel warm.

You won't recall each moment,
the nights I paced the floor,
but I was there in every breath,
I loved you even more.

And one day you'll outgrow me,
in ways I'll understand,
but still, you'll hold my fingerprint
inside your steady hand.

For love like this is quiet,
not showy, loud or grand.
It's built of years and little things,
and holding when you can.

So go and build your galaxies,
make mess, and find your name.
Just know the thread between us
will always stay the same.

When She Forgets to Be Grown

She gets in the car,
hood up,
airPods in,
a silence
you've learned not to take personally.

You talk in soft shapes.
Let the silence stretch out
like a road you don't need to rush down.

And then,
somewhere between
the traffic lights
and a song she doesn't skip,
she starts talking.

Not in full sentences,
not with eye contact,
but it's her. Really her.

She tells you about a teacher she likes,
a girl at school who's being weird,
a dream she had
that made no sense
but stayed with her all day.

You keep your voice level,
your hands on the wheel.
You don't want to spook it.
This is sacred ground.

For a few minutes,
she forgets to be
cool,
grumpy,
twelve.

Emotionally Unavailable, But Make It Poetic

And you forget to worry
about whether you're doing enough.

Because this,
this is everything.
Her choosing to let you in,
without being asked,
without needing anything
except your ears.

You don't say much.
Just nod.
And catch the smile
that sneaks across your face
when she's not looking.

She'll retreat again,
as they all do.
But you'll carry this moment
like treasure.

Because for a while,
she remembered
you're still her safe place.
And you remembered
you always will be.

The Hardest Bit

The house is never louder
than the moment after she leaves.
It's not just quiet,
it's *absence*.
An echo of her laugh
still floating near the fridge.

There's a stray sock in the hallway.
A crisp packet by the sofa.
Half a glass of squash
she didn't finish
because she was too busy
telling me everything
and nothing
at once.

I say,
"See you soon."
Because I don't know
what else to say
that won't unravel me.

Because if I say
"I miss you already,"
she'll look sad.
And I can't be the reason for that.
Not again.

So I smile.
Make it easy.
Wave like it's normal.
Like I'm not already
counting days
backwards.

Emotionally Unavailable, But Make It Poetic

And when the door closes,
I don't cry.
But I do sit down
in the mess we made together
and feel it all at once.

The joy,
the weight,
the guilt that slips in quietly
like a coat you forgot you were wearing.

Being a dad
on borrowed time
teaches you
how to love
in short bursts
and long silences.

So I hold the silence
like it's sacred.
And wait
for the next time
she's here
to fill it again.

You Stayed. I Stayed.
(From someone with bipolar, to the one who stayed)

There are things I don't say,
not because they aren't true,
but because this illness
sometimes steals my voice
and leaves me lost inside a version of myself
even I don't recognise.

But if I could speak it,
I'd say this:

Thank you
for staying
when I swing too high
and burn too bright,
when sleep is a stranger
and my thoughts don't land.

For staying
when I crash so low
that getting out of bed
feels like trying to move the world.

For not flinching
when I'm too much,
and not walking away
when I'm not enough.

You don't always understand,
and I don't expect you to.
But your effort,
your steady presence,
means more than I can ever explain.

Emotionally Unavailable, But Make It Poetic

You see me
beneath the chaos.
You wait
without pressure.
You hold out your hand,
even when I can't reach back.

I know I disappear.
I know I change.
I know it hurts to love someone
who can flip like weather.

But your patience
is the calm between storms.
Your love
makes the hard parts survivable.

I might not always say it.
I might not always show it.
But I see you.

And I'm still here,
because you are.

You Don't See What I See

You say you're a mess.
A walking disaster.
Like the universe just gave up halfway through
and said, "Eh, that'll do."

But you don't see what I see.

You think you're all flaws,
like a scratched-up record nobody plays.
But I hear the music,
even in the skips.
Especially in the skips.

You call yourself clumsy,
tripping over words and pavements alike.
But even falling,
you've got more grace
than you'll ever admit.

And those rosy cheeks you complain about?
The ones you try to hide,
thinking they give you away?
They're warmth in a world so cold.
Proof you're alive,
even when you don't feel it.

You apologise too much,
for breathing, for existing,
for taking up space.
But you *should* take up space.
You should claim it,
decorate it,
make it yours.

Emotionally Unavailable, But Make It Poetic

Because you don't see what I see.

You see imperfections.
I see texture.
You see cracks.
I see the light pouring through them.
You see someone small.
I see someone carrying mountains
like they're made of feathers.

You think you're not enough.
But to me?
You're everything.

So the next time you call yourself
a mess,
a failure,
a burden,
remember this:
I'd rather be lost in your chaos
than perfectly fine anywhere else.

You don't see what I see.
But maybe, just maybe,
you could try.

I'm Proud of You

I'm proud of you.
For getting up when your mind begged you to stay down.
For showing up to the day
when your heart just wasn't in it.

For doing the bare minimum,
because that was *all you had*,
and still calling that enough.

I'm proud of you for being gentle
when it would've been easier to be cruel,
especially to yourself.

For the way you've carried things
that no one else could see.
The worry. The weight. The *what-ifs*.
And still, you kept going.

I know there were nights
where the silence was too loud.
Mornings that arrived before you were ready.
Days that asked too much,
and gave too little in return.

I know you've questioned your worth.
Wondered if you're too much, or not enough.
Held your breath in rooms where you felt out of place.

But look at you.
Still here.
Still trying.

That's not small. That's strength.

So even if no one claps for you today,
even if the world doesn't notice,
I do.

Emotionally Unavailable, But Make It Poetic

Because healing doesn't come with fireworks,
and growth doesn't always look like progress.
Sometimes, it's just getting through the next five minutes.
Sometimes, it's saying "I'll try again tomorrow."

So I'm proud of you.
For the quiet victories.
The invisible wins.
The nights you didn't give up.
The mornings you got back up.

And I hope, one day,
when the dust settles and the noise fades,
you'll look back and feel it too.
Not shame,
Not regret,
But pride.

Because you earned that.

Dogs Are Proof the Universe Got Something Right

Have you ever been loved so hard
you forgot the world was cruel?
That's a dog.
A heartbeat wrapped in fur,
tail wagging like it's powered
by pure, unfiltered joy.

They don't care
how bad your day was,
how messy your hair is,
or that you've been in the same pyjamas
for two days.
To them, you're a hero,
a god,
the centre of their universe.

Their love is ridiculous.
You give them a stick,
they act like you handed them
the crown jewels.
You come back from taking the bins out,
and they greet you like you've returned
from war.

And they forgive.
Oh, do they forgive.
You stepped on their tail once?
They forgot in a second.
You left them alone for hours?
They act like it never happened,
as long as there's belly rubs after.

They speak without words:
a paw on your lap when you're sad,
a head tilt that asks,
"Are you okay, human?"

Emotionally Unavailable, But Make It Poetic

They just *know*.
It's like they're tuned
to the frequency of your soul.

And let's not forget their quirks.
The zoomies at 3 a.m.
The dramatic flop on the floor
when they're being ignored.
The way they somehow always know
when you're holding cheese.

Dogs don't judge.
They don't hold grudges.
They just love.
Unconditionally.
Wholeheartedly.
In a way that makes you wonder
how we got so lucky
to have them at all.

So here's to dogs,
the healers,
the comedians,
the unspoken therapists.

Because in a world
that's often too much,
dogs remind us
what it feels like
to be enough.

Sanctuary on Wheels

I patch the broken, stitch the torn,
Pull life from edges frayed and worn,
In the back of this box, sanctuary bound,
Where the world quiets, patient sounds surround.

I see things no one should see,
Scars they carry, haunting me,
My hands know the rhythm, the beat, the breath,
Yet, I can't shake the shadows or quiet death.

Inside, my walls are tightly sewn,
Stories locked, unshared, unknown,
A healer's mask, each shift I wear,
To keep the silence and the stare.

How can I save others but not myself,
Pull them from darkness while lost in my own hell?
I watch their eyes, the fear, the plea,
As if their lives are pieces of me.

Back to my sanctuary, every night,
With hands that heal but lose their fight,
For each life I save, a part of me goes,
Into the quiet where no one knows.

The Only Way Out

The world won't wait for your breaking.
It won't slow down when you do.
The clocks keep ticking,
the sky stays blue,
even when you're drowning in grey.

No one's coming with a miracle.
No spotlight, no rescue scene.
Your friends might reach,
but it's your grip
that decides if you'll be seen.

Some days, you'll shake.
Some nights, you'll ache.
You'll sit in silence
and call it home.
But even then, especially then,
you're never truly alone.

Because the sun still shows up,
even after the worst of storms.
And if it can rise,
so can you,
battered, but being reborn.

The world might not hold you gently,
but you can choose to care.
To speak to yourself with softness,
to breathe your own repair.

Be the hand that lifts you.
Be the light that cuts through.
You are not beyond saving,
but the one who must save you…
is you.

Emotionally Unavailable, But Make It Poetic

THAT'LL DO

You're still tired, but funnier now.
This section is for the low effort wins and sarcastic survival strategies.
Cancelled plans, crap food, small joys, inner child chaos.
Healing doesn't always look profound.
Sometimes it looks like finally using the good mug.

How to Be a Functioning Adult (According to Me, Who Is Not One)

Step 1: **Wake up before noon.**
(Technically 11:47 counts.)
Do not snooze your alarm seven times.
Snooze it six,
then lie there
reconsidering everything.

Step 2: **Hydrate.**
Start strong with a full water bottle.
Forget it exists by 10am.
Rediscover it at 4pm,
lukewarm and judging you.

Step 3: **Eat three balanced meals.**
Or two.
Or one, but dramatically.
Eat cereal out of a mug
and call it a self-care ritual.

Step 4: **Be productive.**
Make a to-do list so long it becomes a poem.
Do none of it.
Add "make list" to the list
so you can tick it off
and feel something.

Step 5: **Be professional.**
Send emails that say,
"Hope you're well!"
while internally screaming.
End with "Kind regards"
to hide the existential dread.

Step 6: **Keep your house tidy.**
Which means moving piles
from one surface to another.
Bonus points if you light a candle
and pretend it fixes everything.

Step 7: **Budget responsibly.**
Don't buy another novelty mug.
Do not.
…Okay but it says "emotional support beverage."
That's basically therapy.

Step 8: **Exercise.**
Open the fitness app.
Look at the fitness app.
Close the fitness app.
Google "Can you tone your arms by thinking about it?"

Step 9: **Maintain a social life.**
Cancel plans.
Feel guilty.
Rearrange.
Cancel again.
Repeat until you're 40.

Step 10: **Get enough sleep.**
Put your phone down.
Put it *down*.
Watch six TikToks.
Accidentally watch someone's divorce story.
Now you're emotionally invested and it's 2am.

—

And yet.
Somehow.
You're still here.
Still showing up.
Still laughing at the madness of it all.

So maybe that's what being an adult really is:
Just doing your best
with a half-charged phone,
a slightly chaotic mind,
and a fridge that only contains condiments.

Emotionally Unavailable, But Make It Poetic

Congratulations.
You're functioning.
Sort of.

Gold star. ✦

Meal Planning for People Who Can't Be Arsed

Step 1: **Make a plan.**
Write down ambitious meals like
"stir-fried soba noodles with sesame glaze"
and "slow-cooked Moroccan chicken."
Fully knowing you'll end up
eating toast over the sink.

Step 2: **Do a big shop.**
Buy everything you need.
Plus extra things you absolutely don't.
Like five types of cheese.
And one sad courgette
you'll later watch die in slow motion.

Step 3: **Cook Monday's meal.**
Start with enthusiasm.
Play music.
Chop confidently.
Forget one ingredient,
improvise with something strange,
eat it anyway.
Call it rustic.

Step 4: **Tuesday.**
Leftovers.
Cold.
Standing up.
Out of a Tupperware container
that no longer has a lid.
Still counts.

Step 5: **Wednesday.**
Consider cooking.
Feel a deep spiritual fatigue.
Have cereal for dinner.
Tell yourself calcium is important.

Step 6: **Thursday.**
Open the fridge.
Stare at the courgette.
Close the fridge.
Order takeaway.

Step 7: **Friday.**
Clean the fridge out of guilt.
Throw away things you *meant* to use.
Hold a quiet funeral for the feta.
Swear next week will be different.

Step 8: **Saturday.**
You become a raccoon.
Eat odd combinations like
crisps and hummus,
toast and yoghurt,
pasta with… is that ketchup?

Step 9: **Sunday.**
Meal plan again.
Believe in yourself.
Repeat steps 1–8 forever.

—

Because sometimes
feeding yourself isn't about kale
or quinoa
or "macros."

It's about surviving the week
with minimal dishes,
maximum comfort,
and the courage to admit
that a Peperami and a Babybel
is a meal if you eat them
with enough conviction.

Bon appétit, king.

Peace and Potatoes

I don't need enlightenment today.
I just need carbs.
And the kind of quiet
that feels earned.

There's a tray in the oven
and a YouTube video I've watched before.
I know how it ends.
That's why I love it.

The potatoes are nothing special,
frozen,
seasoned with whatever I grabbed first,
probably chili salt.
Always chili salt.

But there's peace in the crunch.
In the little golden edges
that don't judge me
for staying in joggers
or not answering that email
or being just a bit
flat.

Nobody claps when you make oven chips,
but maybe they should.

Maybe surviving the day
without drama
is its own kind of gourmet.

I eat slowly.
Let the quiet settle in.
And for once,
I don't try to turn it into a metaphor.
It's just dinner.
And I'm just... okay.

Which feels like winning.

The Art of Doing Nothing

I woke up at noon, still snug in my bed,
Ignoring the plans that danced in my head.
The hustle can wait; I'm feeling content,
Because time spent happy is time well spent.

Breakfast at one, a gourmet display:
Cereal from the box, it's that kind of day.
The dishes can wait; I've no need to repent,
Because time spent happy is time well spent.

The couch is my throne; I sink into place,
With snacks in my lap and a smile on my face.
They say, "Get up! Be productive, invent!"
But time spent happy is time well spent.

I binged a whole series; it wasn't a chore.
Met fictional friends I now truly adore.
They lifted my mood, made my worries relent,
And proved time spent happy is time well spent.

Dinner was pizza from two nights ago,
Paired with some chocolate I'd hidden below.
The gym can wait; my joy won't ferment,
Because time spent happy is time well spent.

Some call it lazy, but I call it care,
For resting my soul, not gasping for air.
Self-care is an art, my energy well lent,
Because time spent happy is time well spent.

In Defence of Beige Food

(An unranked list of reasons I keep eating like a 7-year-old left home alone)

1. It doesn't ask questions.
2. It never judges.
3. It's already in the freezer.
4. It can be eaten in shame or triumph.
5. Toast is both a meal and a coping mechanism.
6. Beige food doesn't demand sauces it made up in therapy.
7. It's not trying to *cleanse* me.
8. A crisp sandwich once got me through heartbreak.
9. It tastes the same whether you're thriving or spiralling.
10. Nuggets don't care if you haven't been to the gym.
11. Anything golden-brown is basically self-care.
12. It goes with ketchup, which is legally a vegetable.
13. Pasta doesn't need to "pop." It just needs to turn up.
14. Potatoes come in seven comforting forms.
15. You can eat it on the sofa, in bed, or hunched over a sink.
16. You don't need a spiraliser.
17. It's been there for me when kale couldn't be.
18. Beige food understands I'm not looking to be *transformed*.
19. Sometimes I just want to feel full and held.
20. Beige food is a hug I can chew.

The Joy of Cancelling Plans

I don't hate people. I just… love cancelling on them. Not because I didn't want to go. I did, in theory. But the version of me who agreed to it was well-rested and full of optimism. The current version just wants silence, soft lighting, and a reason not to interact with cutlery.

So when you text saying, "Shall we rearrange?" I feel a joy that's hard to explain. It's not laziness. It's relief. A quiet kind that settles across your shoulders and makes the evening stretch ahead like a warm bath.

We'll reschedule. Probably. Eventually. But right now?
I've already mentally committed to not wearing proper trousers.

And honestly,
that feels like the healthiest decision I've made all week.

My Inner Child Is Feral

People say,
"Connect with your inner child."
But mine?
He's unhinged.

He's barefoot,
covered in mud,
holding a stick he swears is Excalibur
and a Capri-Sun he's already stabbed too hard.

He cries when the toast is "wrong."
He laughs when people fall over.
He wants to ride the trolley in Tesco
and scream if we don't buy Mini-Eggs.

He doesn't care about savings,
career goals,
or the fact that we haven't returned that email
from last week.
Or last month.
...Okay, it's been a year.

He wants to chase pigeons,
skip lunch,
and buy things based solely on colour.

He doesn't believe in portion sizes,
bedtimes, or
keeping quiet in public.

And honestly? Sometimes he wins.

Sometimes I eat Wotsits in bed
and blow bubbles in my drink
and spend £24.99 on something I do *not* need
because it looks like a frog.

And it helps.
Not in a profound,
life-altering,
"go to therapy" way.

But in a
"the world is ridiculous so I might as well be too"
kind of way.

So yeah,
I'm trying to befriend the little goblin in me.
Let him pick the cereal sometimes.
Let him draw with the nice pens.
Let him laugh so hard he snorts.

Because being an adult is overrated.
And my inner child?
He might be feral,
but at least he's free.

This Cup of Tea Deserves an Award

It's nothing fancy.
Just a builder's brew in a chipped mug
with a handle that's seen things.

But I swear,
this cup of tea
is the only thing holding me together today.

Not therapy.
Not journaling.
Not self-improvement podcasts hosted by people named Brad.

Just this mug,
a splash of milk,
and five minutes where nobody needs anything from me.

There's something holy about the steam
rising like a tiny miracle,
and the way the tea bag gives up its bitterness
slowly,
like it knows what kind of day I've had.

It doesn't ask questions.
Doesn't offer solutions.
Doesn't tell me "you just need to reframe it."
It just… exists.
Warm, quiet,
patient.

And maybe that's all I needed too.

So yeah,
this cup of tea
wins the award for
Best Supporting Role in My Mental Stability.

Cheers.

My Parking Spot

Someone's in my space again.
Not officially mine, but let's be honest,
we both know it is.
That spot's been mine
since before they even moved in.
It's got tyre marks with my name on them.

Now I'm circling the street
like I've lost something important.
I mutter things
I definitely wouldn't say
if my window was down.

Eventually I park three spaces down,
but it's not the same.
The angle's weird.
The lighting's wrong.
The vibes are off.

I go inside pretending I'm over it.
But I'm not.

I think about that space
at least four more times
before bed.

Nothing Happened Today and That Was Lovely

No drama.
No spirals.
No emotional breakthroughs in the middle of Tesco.
Just… a day.

I woke up without the crushing weight of vague dread.
Didn't achieve much,
but didn't catastrophise either.
A calm, beige kind of peace.

I washed a fork.
Put the washing on.
Didn't open Facebook even once.
(Okay, maybe once. But briefly. And I didn't compare myself to
anyone. Much.)

No major life questions.
No inner child to heal.
No wild urge to reinvent myself
via haircut, houseplant, or impulsive purchase.

Just small, soft things.
A text from someone I like.
A walk where nothing profound happened,
except I noticed a bird
and didn't Google what it meant.

I didn't save the world.
Didn't destroy it either.
And maybe that's enough.

Because not every day needs
a comeback,
a plot twist,
or a life lesson.

Emotionally Unavailable, But Make It Poetic

Some days just need to pass
quietly,
gently,
like this one.

And I think I'll let them.

You're Still Here *(a letter to you)*

You don't have to feel strong right now.
You don't need to smile or glow or rise.
Some days are about survival.
Some days are just about not disappearing.

You're still here.

Even with tired bones
and a mind that won't switch off.
Even with a heart that feels too heavy to carry.

You're still here.

Maybe today didn't feel like living.
Maybe it felt more like enduring.
Like you were dragging yourself through hours
while pretending you were fine.
But you showed up.
In your way.
And that matters more than you know.

Because surviving is not weakness.
It's strength no one claps for.
It's the quiet kind,
the kind that looks like making a cup of tea
when everything hurts.
The kind that gets out of bed
when there's no motivation left,
just muscle memory
and the hope that maybe tomorrow will be softer.

You're still here.

You don't have to have the answers.
You don't have to be full of light.
You just have to keep going,
imperfectly,
gently,
truthfully.

And on the days that feel still,
slow,
silent,
remember this:

You are doing something most people never see.
You are living through something
most people wouldn't understand.

And one day,
when this chapter no longer stings,
you'll look back and realise,
this was the moment you didn't give up.

And that changed everything.

You're still here.
You're still here.
And that's not nothing.
That's *everything*.

People Are Exhausting

People talk too much.
They fill the air with half-formed thoughts,
opinions no one asked for,
small talk that grates like a loose thread on a sweater,
unraveling my patience, one tug at a time.

They walk too slow when I'm in a hurry,
too fast when I need a moment.
They stand in doorways,
block aisles,
exist in places I wish were empty.

People ask questions with answers they won't listen to.
"How are you?" doesn't mean how are you,
it means lie to me, so I don't have to care.
And God forbid you tell the truth,
because now you're "too much."

They invade my space with their noise,
their chewing,
their coughing,
their breathing.
Too loud, too close,
always there.

They make plans they won't keep,
say things they don't mean,
pretend they understand when they don't.
They demand attention, drain energy,
then leave like they were never the problem.

I should live in the woods.
Somewhere quiet.
Where the only voices belong to the wind,
and the only thing blocking the aisle
is a fallen tree that knows how to stay put.

Emotionally Unavailable, But Make It Poetic

Maybe this is the part
where I soften,
where I remind myself that people mean well,
that connection matters,
that solitude is just another kind of loneliness.

But no.
Not today.
Today, I'll just stay annoyed.

Swipe Right…

They say love's a game, but I missed the score,
So here I am swiping, like some digital chore.
Left on the "yogis," the "star sign queens,"
Right on the girls who "love strong caffeine."

Match! We chat, she's got banter for days,
Talking all sorts of "spontaneous ways."
So we meet at a bar, I'm feeling a win,
Till she orders six shots and says, "Let's begin."

Two drinks in, and she's spilling her past,
About wild nights and flings that don't last.
She's into yoga retreats, her "soul's come alive,"
Her "exes were toxic," but hey, she'll survive.

Then she leans in close, with a smirk and a wave,
"Little fun fact, I used to be Dave."

The Algorithm Knows Me Better Than I Do

Swipe.
Another cat video.
Two seconds in,
I'm emotionally invested in Mr. Whiskers
learning to high-five.

Swipe.
A stranger spills their trauma
over lo-fi beats.
I wasn't ready for a therapy session,
but here I am,
nodding like I know their pain.

Swipe.
A DIY hack for a life I don't have.
Apparently, I need to organise my spices.
(I don't even cook.)

Swipe.
Relationship advice from someone
who's single but confident.
"Know your worth!" they yell,
and for a moment, I do.

Swipe.
A thirst trap.
The audacity.
The nerve.
The 3rd replay.

Swipe.
"Things you didn't know you needed on Amazon!"
Now I have a cart full of things
I definitely don't need,
but might order anyway.

Emotionally Unavailable, But Make It Poetic

Swipe.
A dog gets reunited with its owner.
And suddenly, I'm crying at 2 a.m.,
like I know that dog personally.

Swipe.
"Day in the life" of someone
who wakes up at 5 a.m.,
drinks green juice,
and somehow has their life together.
Meanwhile, my laundry's been "airing out"
for three days.

Swipe.
"Stop scrolling!"
But I can't.
Because this app
is a black hole of joy, sadness, and existential dread.
And somehow,
it feels like home.

The algorithm knows me better than I do.
Knows I'll laugh, cry,
and stay up too late,
wondering how I got here.

Swipe.
And just like that,
I forget I was ever lost.

Right on Time

Do you ever feel like you're running late,
Like life is speeding ahead, and you're struggling to catch up?
Like you should be further along,
That you've missed some invisible deadline
For love, success, happiness?

Breathe.

You are not behind.

There is no set age to figure it all out.
No rulebook that says you must have love by 25,
A dream job by 30,
A perfect life by 40.

Some people take the express route,
Others wander through detours and side streets.
But time is not a race,
And your path is yours alone.

The sun doesn't rush to rise,
And the moon never apologises for showing up late.
Yet both arrive exactly when they're meant to.

Growth isn't measured by speed,
But by how deeply you live,
The lessons you learn,
The love you give,
The person you become along the way.

So breathe.
Keep going.
Trust your own pace.

You are not late.
You are not lost.
You are exactly where you need to be.

And if you ever doubt it,
Just look at how far you've already come.

What If Today Was It?

If today was your last day,
how would you spend it?

Would you wake before the world,
just to watch the sunrise paint the sky one final time?
Would you feel the earth beneath your feet,
the breeze against your skin,
and wonder why you didn't stop to notice it more?

Would you call the person who lingers in your mind,
even after all these years?
Would you say the words you were too afraid to before?
Would you hold someone a little longer,
knowing this is the last time you ever will?

Or would you sit in a quiet room,
no screens, no distractions,
just the sound of laughter,
the warmth of the people you love,
letting the moment sink in like never before?

Would you look back and feel at peace?
Or would you wish you had worried less,
lived more,
stopped chasing things that never really mattered?

Because one day, this won't be a question.
One day, time will run out.

And when that moment comes,
you won't be thinking about money,
about titles,
about what strangers thought of you.
You'll be thinking about love.
About the time you had.
About whether you truly made it count.

So why wait for the last day,
to start living this one?

What I've Learnt at 21 (Plus a Few)

I've learnt that plans are more of a *loose suggestion*,
And most people are winging it with quiet aggression.

That sleep is sacred,
social batteries die fast,
And peace is found in staying in, at last.

I've learnt that "Let's catch up soon"
is adult code for "probably never,"
And the friends who stay
don't need constant tether.

I've learnt that anxiety loves 2am,
And that nothing good happens
after re-reading your own texts again.

That loving someone doesn't mean they'll stay,
And not all people who leave were meant to anyway.

I've learnt that healing isn't a mountain,
It's a spiral staircase you sometimes trip down
right after saying "I'm fine."

That therapy is expensive,
but so is pretending you're okay,
Just in different currencies.

I've learnt to stop chasing closure,
because sometimes the closure
is that they were just a bit rubbish.

That time doesn't heal everything,
but it *does* make most things less loud.

I've learnt that joy is often in the small stuff:
Clean sheets.
A cup of tea you didn't make.
A message that says "Made me think of you."

Emotionally Unavailable, But Make It Poetic

I've learnt that people pleasers aren't kind,
they're scared.
And boundaries aren't rude,
they're self-respect, quietly declared.

I've learnt that the older I get,
the less tolerance I have for people
who drain, complain, or overexplain.
(Or chew loudly.)

I've learnt that the world won't end
if someone doesn't like me.
(Still slightly inconvenient, though.)

That "success" doesn't look like it used to,
and "enough" isn't measured in numbers.

I've learnt that rest is productive.
That growing older is a privilege.
And that sometimes,
the bravest thing I'll do all day
is open the curtains.

I've learnt that I need social media less…
but still open it like a fridge,
hoping something new has appeared.

And if I could tell my younger self one thing,
I probably wouldn't.
He'd just ignore me anyway.

Left Sock

Where?
WHY.
What do you know?
Come back.

Thanks for Coming Round

I didn't think you'd stay this long.
Was half-expecting you to skim a few lines,
close the book,
and call it "relatable."

But here you are,
at the end of it all,
after the socks,
the sadness,
and the kitchen-sink metaphors.

I wish I could offer some conclusion,
something profound,
or at least poetic.
But mostly I'm just glad you came.

Glad you read the things
I didn't know how to say out loud.
Glad you didn't flinch
at the soft parts.
Glad you didn't laugh
at the wrong parts
(or maybe you did, and that's okay too).

I don't have advice.
Just… solidarity.
And maybe a spare cuppa,
if you're sticking around.

You don't have to go back
and be fixed, or fine,
or even functional.

You just have to go back and be you.

Maybe with a little more softness this time.

And if not,
there's always page one.

ABOUT THE AUTHOR

Tim Stoodley is a paramedic, poet, and professional overthinker.

He lives in the UK, drinks far too much tea, and writes poems about mental health, grief, fatherhood, cancelled plans, and whatever else his brain decides to spiral over.

This is his first collection. *He's still not sure how he feels about that.*

He also reads poems into his phone and posts them on TikTok: *@poems.by.tim* - It's like performance art, if performance art involved overthinking, poor lighting, and his sofa in the background.

Emotionally Unavailable, But Make It Poetic

Printed in Great Britain
by Amazon

61440711R00060